Arthur C. (Arthur Cayley) Headlam

The Teaching of the Russian Church

Arthur C. (Arthur Cayley) Headlam

The Teaching of the Russian Church

ISBN/EAN: 9783744665278

Printed in Europe, USA, Canada, Australia, Japan

Cover: Foto ©Lupo / pixelio.de

More available books at **www.hansebooks.com**

THE

Teaching of the Russian Church

BEING NOTES ON POINTS ON WHICH
IT DIFFERS FROM THE ENGLISH CHURCH

BY

ARTHUR C. HEADLAM, B.D.

RECTOR OF WELWYN, HERTS

FORMERLY FELLOW OF ALL SOULS' COLLEGE, OXFORD

PUBLISHED FOR

THE EASTERN CHURCH ASSOCIATION

RIVINGTONS

KING STREET, COVENT GARDEN

LONDON

1897

PREFACE

THE following Paper was read originally before a Society of East London Clergy, and is now published on the advice of several friends, in a somewhat enlarged form, and with a few necessary alterations.

The Paper can naturally make no pretence to completeness. It has two purposes. The first is to give, in the language of authorised documents, or of writers who may be regarded as representative interpreters of their Church, the teaching of the Russian Church on those subjects particularly about which questions might be asked, namely those points on which its teaching differs from that of our own Church, or of the Church of Rome, or those on which controversy and discussion have been raised.

The second purpose is to try and bring out what the writer believes to be the temper and spirit of the Russian Church. Two Churches may have exactly the same offices and professions of Faith, and yet their life and spirit may be quite different. The same beliefs may be held in very different ways.

It has been thought convenient to add at the end a short list of the service books and authorised doctrinal statements of the Russian Church, and of translations of them into English, with a few books, accessible to English readers, on the Russian Church.

It has been thought advisable in some points to contrast the teaching of the Russian Church with that of Rome. That form of Roman teaching has been selected which is most commonly presented to us, and imitated by members of our own Church. Historically, Rome has much more in common with the East, but unfortunately the historical side of Rome's teaching is that which we are least allowed to see.

A. C. H.

THE TEACHING
OF THE RUSSIAN CHURCH

THE Russian Church is, as is well known, a branch—
by far the largest and most important branch—of the
Orthodox Eastern Church, the Holy Synod, which is its
governing body, having the authority of a Patriarch,
and the Church being an independent Patriarchate
on the same footing as the older Patriarchates of Constantinople, Antioch, Alexandria, and Jerusalem.

The Eastern Church professes to be the only true
Church, both Catholic and Orthodox, and in its general
position is strongly anti-Roman in the sense of protest-
ing with great vigour against the uncatholic and un-
historical claims of the Pope.

Speaking broadly, it bases its claims to be the Catholic
and Orthodox Church on the acceptance of:—

 (1.) Holy Scripture.
 (2.) The Niceno-Constantinopolitan Creed.
 (3.) The Seven General Councils.
 (4.) The Seven Sacraments.

In the following pages an attempt will be made to
illustrate its teaching on certain points selected, not for
their actual, but for their controversial importance.
They represent either those doctrines which have
unfortunately been subjects of controversy between

A

different Christian bodies, or those about which discussion exists at the present time.

The two principal documents used are *The Longer
Catechism of the Russian Church*, and *The Treatise on
the Duty of Parish Priests*. The former, although
based on older documents, is, as it at present stands,
the work of Archbishop Philaret, the well-known Metropolitan of Moscow, and was promulgated by the Holy
Synod in 1839. It was translated into Greek, and
sent to the Eastern Patriarchs. *The Treatise on the
Duty of Parish Priests* was first printed at St. Petersburg, in A.D. 1776. It is used by the whole Russian
Church, and all candidates for Holy Orders are required
to have read it, and to show their acquaintance with
its contents. Both these documents are quoted in a
translation published by the Rev. W. Blackmore in
1845.[1]

With regard to the latter, it may be remarked that
it represents an admirable compendium of priestly
duties. There is a general idea current in England
that the clergy of all other churches, and especially
those of the Eastern Church, are, compared with our
own clergy, miserably educated. Such judgments of
others are always unjust and arrogant, and certainly
many candidates for Orders in the Church of England
would gain greatly by possessing an authorised manual
such as this, from which to learn their duties.

Both these documents are, in a sense, authoritative

---

[1] *The Doctrine of the Russian Church*, by the Rev. R. W. Blackmore, B.A., formerly of Merton College, Oxford. Aberdeen, A. Brown
and Co. 1845.

publications, but they have no symbolical authority. The Eastern Church has no general doctrinal tests beyond the Creed itself.

' As regards the question of doctrinal authority generally, it is important to understand that the members of the Eastern Church are neither bound in conscience, on the one hand, to every word and letter of any modern documents, nor left free, on the other hand, to indulge in an unlimited licence of criticism. Beyond the Creed itself, the Eastern Church has no general doctrinal tests ; no Oath, like that of Pope Pius IV. ; no Symbolical Books, strictly speaking, like those of the Protestants and the Reformed ; no Thirty-nine Articles, like those subscribed in England. But still she is not the less on that account provided with a sufficient security that the true faith, in its fullest sense, shall be held and taught under the letter of the Creed, and that the doctrinal decisions of former ages shall be maintained. This security lies in a living spirit of orthodoxy, protected against gainsayers, in case of necessity, by the terror of excommunication. Whatever is felt or known to form part of the faith of the Church, even though it be as yet unwritten, must be received with implicit veneration, as coming from the infallible Spirit of God : much more all doctrine of faith which has been written by orthodox men, or even by whole Synods, so far as it is felt and known to have the sanction of the Church.'[1]

Reference is occasionally made to other documents, and to illustrate the more authorised statements much use has been made of the works of the well-known Russian writer, A. S. Khomiakoff. *L'Église et le Protestantisme au point de vue de l'Église d'Orient* was published at Lausanne in 1872, while his correspondence with Mr. Palmer, and his Essay on the Church,

---

[1] Blackmore, *op. cit.* p. viii.

have been translated for the Eastern Church Association.[1]

In order to prevent an erroneous idea which might arise from the special subjects here touched upon, that, in the teaching of the Russian Church, there is any false sense of proportion, and that what we rightly call the Evangelical doctrines are not taught, it may be noticed that the true proportion of the Christian faith is very apparent in both the official documents with which we are concerned. In the instructions to parish priests, for example, under the heading of 'What the priest ought to teach, and whence,' it is said :—

'It is the priest's duty to teach his flock the Faith and the Law ; the word law being used for the good works of the law. These two things Christ Himself taught, and began His preaching thus : *Repent ye, and believe the Gospel* (Mark i. 15). And the Apostle Paul in like manner taught both Jews and Greeks *repentance towards God, and faith towards our Lord Jesus Christ* (Acts xx. 21). To repentance belong the works of the law, to the Gospel, faith in Christ.'

Of the faith it is said :—

'The Faith consists in divers Articles, which Christians must believe and confess ; of which some are principal, and so necessary to salvation, that without the knowledge of them a man cannot be saved, any more than he can live without the principal members of the body, as the head, the heart, and the like ; while others, especially for simple people busied with their worldly callings, are less necessary,

---

[1] *Russia and the English Church during the last Fifty Years*, vol. i., by W. J. Birkbeck. Published for the Eastern Church Association. London, Rivington, Percival, and Co., 1895. Of M. Khomiakoff himself a full account is given in the Preface to the latter work.

as being implied in the first, and belonging only to their more exact statement and explanation.

'To the first class of Articles belongs the mystery of the Holy Trinity; the mission of the Son of God into the world; our Justification by His Death; God's mercy to fallen man, and His Grace leading to repentance; and the like.'

'All the Articles of the Faith are contained in the Word of God, that is, in the Books of the Old and New Testaments.'

'The Law of the Ten Commandments is likewise contained in Holy Scripture, in the twentieth chapter of Exodus; and since it is innate in us, and the mirror of that Image of God in which man was created, it follows that every Christian, without exception, is most certainly required to know it, and to lead his life by it, doing good works, and eschewing evil.'[1]

We may pass on now to the teaching concerning the Sacraments. The Russian Church recognises and considers essential to a true Church seven Sacraments or Mysteries, viz.: 'Baptism, Unction with Chrism, Communion, Penitence, Orders, Matrimony, Unction with Oil.'

A mystery or sacrament is defined as 'a holy act, through which *grace*, or, in other words, the saving power of God, works *mysteriously* upon man.'

'In Baptism man is mysteriously born to a spiritual life. In Unction with Chrism he receives a grace of spiritual growth and strength. In the Communion he is spiritually fed. In Penitence he is healed of spiritual diseases, that is, of sin. In Orders he receives grace spiritually to regenerate, feed, and nurture others, by doctrine and Sacraments. In

---

[1] *A Treatise on the Duty of Parish Priests*, translated by Rev. R. W. Blackmore, pp. 159-161.

Matrimony he receives a grace sanctifying the married life, and the natural procreation and nurture of children. In Unction with Oil he has medicine even for bodily diseases, in that he is healed of spiritual.'[1]

Of the Sacraments generally, it is said :—

'It is the Priest's duty before he administers any Sacrament to teach him who desires to receive it, if he be ignorant, what is the virtue of the same Sacrament. . . . For if he, to whom the Sacrament is administered, be left uninstructed of this, he will not know himself what he receives; consequently, neither can he have faith, which naturally follows only upon the knowledge of what is to be believed; and so he will not receive that grace of God, which is given in the Sacrament : *for our faith alone is the hand by which we receive all those gifts of God, which have been obtained for us by our Lord Jesus Christ.*'[2]

We may now pass on to the Doctrine of the Holy Eucharist. It will be most convenient to begin by some extracts from the Longer Catechism of the Russian Church.

'*Q.* What is the Communion ?

'*A.* The Communion is a Sacrament in which the believer, under the forms of bread and wine, partakes of the very Body and Blood of Christ, to everlasting life.

'*Q.* What is the most essential act in this part of the Liturgy (*i.e.* in the Liturgy of the faithful).

'*A.* The utterance of the words which Jesus Christ spoke in instituting the Sacrament : Take, eat, this is My Body; Drink ye all of it, for this is My Blood of the New Testament, Matt. xxvi. 26, 27, 28. And after this, the invocation of the Holy Ghost, and the

---

[1] *The Longer Catechism*, Blackmore, p. 84.
[2] *Duty of Parish Priests*, Blackmore, p. 204.

blessing the gifts, that is, the bread and wine, which have been offered.

'*Q.* Why is this so essential ?

'*A.* Because at the moment of this act the bread and wine are changed, or transubstantiated, into the very Body of Christ, and into the very Blood of Christ.

'*Q.* How are we to understand the word *Transubstantiation* ?

'*A.* In the exposition of the faith by the Eastern Patriarchs, it is said that the word transubstantiation is not to be taken to define the manner in which the bread and wine are changed into the Body and Blood of the Lord, for this none can understand but God; but only thus much is signified, that the bread truly, really, and substantially becomes the very true Body of the Lord, and the wine the very true Blood of the Lord.'

And then comes a quotation from St. John of Damascus :—

'It is truly that Body united with the Godhead, which had its origin from the Holy Virgin : not as though that Body which ascended came down from heaven, but because the bread and wine themselves are changed into the Body and Blood of God. But if thou seekest after the manner how this is, let it suffice thee to be told, that it is by the Holy Ghost, in like manner as by the same Holy Ghost the Lord formed flesh to Himself, and in Himself, from the Mother of God ; nor know I aught more than this, that the word of God is true, powerful, and almighty, but in its manner of operation unsearchable.'—IV. xiii. 7.

'*Q.* What benefit does he receive who communicates in the Body and Blood of Christ ?

'*A.* He is in the closest manner united to Jesus Christ Himself, and in Him is made partaker of everlasting Life.'[1]

---

[1] *The Longer Catechism*, Blackmore, pp. 91-92.

The first point that we notice is, that the word
Transubstantiation is used; and this is quite clearly
and definitely part of the authorised teaching of the
Eastern Church. But when once that is admitted, it
becomes apparent that it is not used in the Roman
sense.[1] That this is so, is shown by a study of the Acts

---

[1] Since the above was written, the following quotation from a
Russian periodical, which appeared in the *Guardian* of May 12th,
1897, puts the Russian objection to Roman doctrine very much more
strongly than is done in the text; It may be noted that the whole
question is at present the subject of a discussion in Russian magazines.

THE VIEWS OF THE METROPOLITAN PHILARET OF MOSCOW UPON THE
LATIN DOCTRINE OF TRANSUBSTANTIATION.

Under the above heading the official journal of the St. Petersburg
Ecclesiastical Academy, the *Tzerkovny Viéstnik (Church Messenger)*
of March 27th (April 8th) contains an account of a conversation held
between the former Bishop of New York, Dr. Young, and the famous
Metropolitan Philaret of Moscow, which, in view of a recent discussion which took place in our columns, will be read with interest by
many of our readers. The interview between Dr. Young and the
Metropolitan Philaret took place during the visit of the former to
Russia in the early sixties, a few years before the death of Philaret
in 1867 :—

'Upon Dr. Young putting some questions with regard to the use of the
word Transubstantiation in the Russian Church, the Metropolitan Philaret
answered in substance as follows :—"This word was introduced into Russia
through Kieff in the seventeenth century, by means of the Roman Catholic
theological literature which was then imported thither." [N.B.—At that
time Kieff was still in the hands of the Poles, and every possible means were
being taken to Latinise the Orthodox population of that part of Russia.]
"Since that time some of our theologians have adopted it, but others very
strongly disapprove of it. I myself belong decidedly to the latter class.
The manner of our Lord's presence in the Blessed Eucharist is a mystery to
be apprehended by faith, and not a matter to be speculated and dogmatised
upon, or to be reasoned about. All definitions or pretended explanations,
such as the use of the word Transubstantiation (*Transsubstantziatzija*), are
nothing but attempts to penetrate into the mystery, and thereby they over-
throw the essence of a sacrament."

'"But," said Dr. Young, "is not the word Transubstantiation used in
your Longer Catechism?"

'"No," replied Philaret with emphasis, "it is not. In Russian we say

of the Synod of Bethlehem, or—as it is sometimes called—of Jerusalem. This Synod was held in the year 1672, at a time when the Eastern Church was largely under Roman influence, and represents that one of the authorised formulæ of the Church which approaches nearest to Roman teaching. In 1838, but not till then, these Acts were translated into Russian.[1]

But in a considerable number of ways their language was changed, and all the more distinctly Roman expressions were taken out. In particular, all reference to the 'accidents' is omitted; for example, where the Russian says:—

'We believe that though the Body and Blood of our Lord

[not *transsubstantziatzija*, but] *presushchestvlénie*, a word corresponding exactly to the Greek word μετουσίωσις."

"'But," said Dr. Young, "it is used more than once by Blackmore in his translation of the Russian Catechism."

'"In that case," replied the Metropolitan, "the translation is incorrect. We have taken good care that the word should not appear in our Catechism."

'This conversation, described by Dr. Young, is extremely interesting, as showing the extraordinary acuteness of our famous Metropolitan's theological intellect, in thus finding a means of preserving the Orthodox teaching concerning μετουσίωσις (*presushchestvlénie*) from the irruption into it of the coarse metaphysics of the schoolmen, with their self-made and, even from a philological point of view, unnatural term, *Transsubstantiatio*.'

We may add that the word *presushchestvlénie* is the exact Slavonic equivalent of the Greek μετουσίωσις, the Slavonic word *sushchestvo* philologically corresponding not to *substantia*, but to οὐσία (*essentia*), and being formed in just the same way from *sushchi*, present participle of the verb *bytj*, to be. When it is remembered that the Metropolitan Philaret was himself the author both of the Longer Catechism and of the translation of the Articles of the Synod of Jerusalem in the form in which the Holy Synod of Russia finally accepted them, it will be difficult to exaggerate the importance of this conversation, and of the fact that it has been reprinted just at this time in one of the leading ecclesiastical journals of Russia.

[1] *See* J. M. Neale, *History of the Holy Eastern Church*, vol. ii. p. 1173.

are divided and separated, yet this takes place in the mystery of the Communion only with respect to the species of bread and wine by which alone they may be seen or touched.'

The Greek has it :—

'The Body and Blood of our Lord are divided and separated by hands and teeth in their accidents alone, and in their accidents of bread and wine.'

The object clearly is to avoid accepting the scholastic philosophy, which is implied in such phraseology; and all that is implied in this is shown by the following extract from Khomiakoff's essay on the Church :—

'She does not reject the word "transubstantiation"; *but she does not assign to it that material meaning which is assigned to it by the teachers of the Churches which have fallen away.* The change of the bread and wine into the Body and Blood of Christ is accomplished in the Church and for the Church. If a man receive the consecrated gifts, or worship them, or think on them with faith, he verily receives, adores, and thinks on the Body and Blood of Christ. If he receive unworthily he verily rejects the Body and Blood of Christ; in any case, in faith or in unbelief he is sanctified or condemned by the Body and Blood of Christ. But this Sacrament is in the Church, and for the Church; not for the outside world, not for fire, not for irrational creatures, not for corruption, and not for the man who has not heard the law of Christ. In the Church itself (we are speaking of the visible Church), to the elect and to the reprobate the Holy Eucharist is not a mere commemoration concerning the mystery of redemption, it is not a presence of spiritual gifts within the bread and wine, it is not merely a spiritual reception of the Body and Blood of Christ, but is His true Body and Blood. Not in spirit alone was Christ pleased to unite Himself with the faithful, but also in Body and in Blood; in order that that union might be complete, and not only spiritual but also corporal.'[1]

---

[1] *Russia and the English Church*, p. 207.

This extract will help to illustrate what underlies the discussion about a word. If transubstantiation or μετουσίωσις or any similar word be used to guard the doctrine of a real Sacramental Presence in the Eucharist, it would express adequately the teaching of the Russian Church; but if the use of the word is supposed to mean the acceptance of the Roman doctrine represented by it, then the word is misleading. The reality of the sacramental teaching of the Russian Church is undoubted, but equally strong is its rejection of the materialised doctrine of the Roman Church.

The language used in authorised books on the subject of the Eucharistic Sacrifice is, in accordance with patristic language. For instance, in the *Duty of Parish Priests*, it is said:—

'More especially is earnest prayer required of the Priest in the service of the Divine Liturgy; for herein not only is that Mystery performed which Christ instituted at His last and mystical Supper, but also the whole economy of our salvation, wrought out by our Lord Jesus Christ, the Son of God, is commemorated, according to the commandment, This do in remembrance of Me.'[1]

So in reference to Prayers for the Dead (of which I shall say more later) allusion is especially made to 'such as are offered in union with the oblation of the Bloodless Sacrifice of the Body and Blood of Christ,'[2] and then a passage from St. Cyril of Jerusalem is quoted: 'Very great will be the benefit to those souls for which prayer is offered at the moment when the holy and tremendous Sacrifice is lying in view.'

---

[1] *The Duty of Parish Priests*, Blackmore, p. 283.
[2] *The Longer Catechism*, Blackmore, p. 99.

The general meaning of the sacrificial language must be gathered from the Liturgy itself, which is, as is well known, the Greek Liturgy. In the Liturgy of St. Chrysostom there is:—

(1.) The prayer of the faithful immediately after the dismissal of the Catechumens, in which the Priest prays: 'Make us to become worthy to offer to Thee prayers and supplications and unbloody sacrifices on behalf of all Thy people.'

(2.) In the prayer before the offertory, the Priest prays for himself that he may be held fit that 'by me Thy sinful and unworthy servant, these gifts may be offered. For Thou art He that offereth and art offered, that receiveth and art given, O Christ.'

(3.) Immediately after the recital of the words of institution, at the invocation, the Priest prays: 'Remembering therefore this saving command, and all things done for us, the cross, the tomb, the resurrection on the third day, the ascension into heaven, the sitting on the right hand, the second and glorious coming, we offer to Thee Thine own (τὰ σὰ ἐκ τῶν σῶν), in all things and for all things, we praise Thee, we bless Thee, we give thanks to Thee, we beseech Thee, our God, and we offer to Thee this reasonable and unbloody service (λατρείαν), and we beseech Thee, and entreat and supplicate Thee, send down Thy Holy Ghost upon us and upon these gifts lying before Thee, and make this bread the precious Body of Thy Christ, and that in this cup, the precious Blood of Thy Christ.'

(4.) The intercession begins, 'And also we offer to Thee this reasonable service on behalf of those who have gone to rest in faith.'

I will conclude these extracts, which are, I think, necessary for our purpose, by one from a work of Khomiakoff's which will, I hope, shortly be translated.

He is describing the difference between the worship of his own Church, and that of the Protestants and the Romans. Of the one he speaks of the coldness; of the other he says, 'A wretched theory of terrestrial diplomacy, extended to the invisible world, has come to replace the faith in the organic unity of the Church.' Of his own Church he says—

'The man thus (by faith and love) united to Christ is no longer what he was, an isolated individual, he is become a member of the Church which is the body of Christ, and his life is become an integral part of that higher life to which he has so freely submitted himself. The Saviour lives in the Church, He lives in us. He intercedes, and it is we who pray : He recommends us to the Divine Favour, and it is we who mutually recommend ourselves to the Creator : He offers Himself in eternal sacrifice, and it is we who present to the Father this sacrifice of glorification, of gratitude and of propitiation, for ourselves and for all our brothers, whether they are still engaged in the dangers of terrestrial conflict or whether death has made them already pass into a condition of serene upward movement.'

I might multiply extracts, but I think that those which I have given, taken partly from authorised formulæ and partly from popular religious writings, are sufficient to let us see something of the belief and temper of the Russian Church in contrast both to that of Rome and to many theologians among ourselves. This difference may be, I think, summed up somewhat as follows :—

1. The Russian and the Eastern Church generally avoid, as much as possible, definition. The Roman Church is always trying to define the manner of the

change in the Sacraments: the Eastern Church says it
is a mystery.   The tendency of the rest of the Western
Christian world has been to try and define what it
does not believe.   The Eastern Church possesses much
more the tone of the early fathers: an intense reality
and boldness of belief; the building up of the service
in the words and language of Scripture; an absence
of rigidity and exactness of language, where human
language is felt to be inadequate and unnecessary.

2. The Russian Church avoids the obtrusively
'priestly' language of the modern Roman Church.
'Did they,' says Cardinal Vaughan, 'claim the power
to produce the actual living Christ Jesus by transubstantiation upon the altar, according to the claims of
the priesthood of the Eastern and Western Churches?'
I do not know whether this exceedingly crude language
would be accepted by modern Roman Catholic theologians: it certainly has a very different ring to that of
the Russian Church.   In their instructions to Parish
Priests they say: 'Before giving the communion of the
most holy Body and Blood of Christ, the Priest should
duly instruct them that wish to communicate, that
This, the Body and Blood of Christ, is not only in name
what it is called, but also verily and indeed is His
Body and His Blood, under the forms of bread and
wine: *for that which consummates this Sacrament is
the operation of the Holy Ghost, to Whom nothing is
impossible.*'   The Roman language speaks of the power
of the Priest, the Russian of the prayers of the Priest
and the work of the Holy Ghost.

3. The Roman Church dissociates the Priest from

the Church, the Eastern associates him with it. How much this is so any one can see who studies the structure of the Eastern services. So the Sacraments are in and for the Church. 'The seven sacraments are not in reality accomplished by any single individual who is worthy of the mercy of God, but by the whole Church in the person of one individual, even though he be unworthy.'[1] This is the teaching which probably most of us have learned through the best English work on the Church and the ministry, and perhaps we are surprised to find it put before us so definitely in the far East. How wonderfully this theory influences all the teaching of the Church may be seen by the book on the duty of the Parish Priests, where the true proportion of the Christian ministry is preserved, as it is in the Encyclical of the English Archbishops.

In reference to Baptism, it is worth while to quote the Baptismal formula, as illustrating one of the points mentioned above. It is as follows:—

'N. The servant of God is baptized in the Name of the Father.—Amen. And of the Son.—Amen. And of the Holy Ghost.—Amen. Now and ever, world without end.— Amen.'

This brings out very clearly what was said above about the manner in which the Orthodox Church avoids 'priestly' language. There are several of our formulæ, derived from Latin sources, to which it would object that they exalt too much the authority of the Priest. This might be further illustrated by the Ordination offices.

As it has sometimes been thought that the Russian

---

[1] Khomiakoff, *Russia and the English Church*, p. 206.

Church does not recognise Western Baptism, it is worth while quoting an authoritative statement on the subject :—

'There are some ignorant men among the clergy who would re-baptize Romans, as well as Lutherans and Calvinists, when they come over to the Eastern Church; while the schismatics among ourselves are not ashamed even to re-baptize those of their people who fall away from the Church, in order to go over to their errors. But the seventh canon of the second Œcumenical Council sufficiently refutes both the ignorance of the first and the blindness of the last : for that holy Council, in the canon cited, forbids to re-baptize not only such as the Romans, Lutherans, and Calvinists (who all clearly confess the Holy Trinity, and admit the work of our salvation accomplished by the Incarnation of the Son of God), but even the Arians themselves.' [1]

On the future state and prayers for the dead, the Catechism teaches :—

' *Q.* In what state are the souls of the dead till the general resurrection ?

' *A.* The souls of the righteous are in light and rest, with a foretaste of eternal happiness ; but the souls of the wicked are in a state the reverse of this.

' *Q.* Why may we not ascribe to the souls of the righteous perfect happiness immediately after death ?

' *A.* Because it is ordained that the perfect retribution

---

[1] *Duty of Parish Priests.* Blackmore, p. 209. See also Birkbeck on *Russia and the English Church,* vol. i. p. 63, where a full history of the Eastern custom with regard to re-baptism is given. The custom of re-baptizing Westerns has been in practice surrendered within the last five-and-twenty years, by both the Church in Greece and the Patriarchate of Constantinople.

Whether the other Patriarchates have followed the example set by these two in their Churches, I do not know.

according to works shall be received by the perfect man, after the resurrection of the body and God's last judgment.

'*Q.* Why do we ascribe to the souls of the righteous a foretaste of bliss before the last judgment?

'*A.* On the testimony of Jesus Christ Himself, who says in the parable that the righteous Lazarus was immediately after death carried into Abraham's bosom.

'*Q.* What is to be remarked of such souls as have departed with faith, but without having had time to bring forth fruits worthy of repentance?

'*A.* This; that they may be aided towards the attainment of a blessed resurrection by prayers offered in their behalf, especially such as are offered in union with the oblation of the Bloodless Sacrifice of the Body and Blood of Christ, and by works of mercy done in faith for their memory.'[1]

The Russian Church does not believe in Purgatory. As Archbishop Philaret (who drew up the Catechism in its present form), wrote:—

'The condition of a man's soul after death is fixed by his internal state; and there is no such thing as Purgatory, in which souls have to pass through fiery torments, in order to prepare them for blessedness. . . . There is no need of any other kind of purification when "the Blood of Jesus Christ cleanseth us from all sin."'

And Khomiakoff writes:[2]—

'We pray for the living that the grace of God may be upon them, and for the dead that they may become worthy of the vision of God's Face. We know nothing of an intermediate

---

[1] *Catechism*, Blackmore, pp. 98, 99.
[2] See *Comparative Statement of Russo-Greek and Roman Catholic Doctrines*, in Papers of the Russo-Greek Committee, No. IV.

state of souls, which have neither been received into the kingdom of God, nor condemned to torture, for of such a state we have received no teaching either from the Apostles or from Christ; we do not acknowledge Purgatory, that is, the purification of souls by sufferings from which they may be redeemed by their own works or those of others ; for the Church knows nothing of salvation by outward means, nor any sufferings whatever they may be, except those of Christ ; nor of bargaining with God, as in the case of a man buying himself off by good works. . . . We pray in the spirit of love, knowing that no one will be saved otherwise than by the prayer of all the Church, in which Christ lives, knowing and trusting that so long as the end of time has not come, all the members of the Church, both living and departed, are being perfected incessantly by mutual prayer.'[1]

It seems to me to be of particular importance to dwell on this teaching at the present time. It is recognised that prayers for the departed have never been condemned by the English Church, and it is felt that the coldness and hardness of what may be called our traditional customs in that matter want correction. There is a natural tendency, especially for the more ignorant, to turn to the one system which lies clearly opened before us, and some are inclined to take over wholesale the modern Roman doctrine and practice concerning Purgatory. I venture to think that this is very much to be lamented. That system has had most deplorable practical developments; it is certainly alien to the whole spirit of early Christianity for centuries; it is a late and corrupt growth. On the other hand, we know that the custom of praying for the departed dates from the very beginning of Christianity, that it finds a

---

[1] *Russia and the English Church*, vol. i. p. 217.

regular place in all Liturgies, and answers to the needs
of the human heart. The teaching that we have quoted
gives a perfectly consistent basis for this, and deserves
our most careful attention.

I do not want to dwell too much on controversial
points, but it is perhaps necessary to remind you that
you will often be told that the Russian Church does
teach Purgatory, and the Synod of Bethlehem will be
quoted. This is another of the passages where the
text of the articles of that Synod was altered before
being circulated in Russia.

On the Invocation of Saints, the Russian Church
teaches as follows :—

'*Q*. What means of communion has the Church on earth
with the Church in heaven ?

'*A*. The prayer of faith and love. The faithful who belong
to the Church militant upon earth, in offering their
prayers to God, call at the same time to their aid the
Saints who belong to the Church in heaven ; and
these, standing on the highest steps of approach to
God, by their prayers and intercessions, purify,
strengthen, and offer before God the prayers of the
faithful living upon earth, and by the will of God
work graciously and beneficently upon them, either
by invisible virtue, or by distinct apparitions, and in
divers other ways.'[1]

This is the official teaching, and it is very carefully
guarded. The fact that all the Saints are prayed for in
the Liturgy, including the Blessed Virgin, is significant.
And Archbishop Philaret tells us that 'No one has
the power to deliver sinners from torments by the

---

[1] *Catechism*, Blackmore, p. 78.

application of the works of *supererogation*, of Jesus
Christ and of the Saints: because the merits of Jesus
Christ are not under the control of man; and works of
supererogation in the Saints are impossible, as they
themselves are only saved by grace.'[1]

What is implied is, that the whole company of the
faithful in heaven and earth are one. United to one
another in the Communion of Saints, the prayers of the
whole Church ascend to heaven on behalf of all; as we
are benefited by the prayers of the living, so are we
benefited by the prayers of those who have gone before.
As we are benefited by the love of the living, so are we
benefited by the love of the departed. And the whole
Church is ever striving to rise upward. Beings who
are not perfect must continually be striving after greater
and greater sanctification, and the departed are in a
state of 'serene upward progress.'[2]

---

[1] Archbishop Philaret, *Comparative Statement, etc.*, p. 16.

[2] In the excellent little work by the Rev. George Body, on *The
Present State of the Faithful Departed*, he writes (p. 50): 'This belief
of the intercession of the Saints does not involve the practice of direct
invocation. Throughout I am using the term *Saints* to designate the
whole company of those who are with Jesus in Paradise. *To invoke
these with direct invocation has never been the wont of any portion of
Catholic Christendom: no one has ever prayed to his mother or to his
friends.*' This statement is incorrect. The practice mentioned is the
habitual custom of the Russian Church. So in the poem of Khomiakoff
on his dead children:—

> 'Dear children, at that same still midnight do ye,
> As I once prayed for you, now in turn pray for me;
> Me who loved well the Cross on your foreheads to trace;
> Now commend me in turn to the mercy and grace
> Of our gracious and merciful God.'
>
> *Russia and the English Church*, Birkbeck, p. 2.

Often, when a child who has lost its mother is praying, he may be
heard adding her name to those of the other saints whom he asks to
pray for him. Mutual prayer of the dead for the living, of the living

On some other points I will now give, as shortly as I can, the teaching of the Russian Church.

On Eikons, it is said: 'We ought to honour them, but not to make Gods of them: for Eikons are merely representations, which serve to remind us of the works of God and His Saints, to the intent that we, by looking upon them, may be stirred up to the imitation of holiness.'

On Chrism, the language is very frank and definite. To the question, 'Is the outward form of unction with Chrism mentioned in Holy Scripture?' it is answered: 'It may well be supposed that the words of St. John (1 John ii. 20, 27), refer to a visible as well as to an inward unction; but it is more certain that the Apostles, for imparting to the baptized the Gifts of the Holy Ghost, used *imposition of hands*, Acts viii. 15, 17. The successors of the Apostles, however, in spite of this, introduced unction with Chrism, deducing, it may be, their precedent from the unction used in the Old Testament.' [1]

The definition of Knowledge and Faith is very interesting—

'Knowledge has for its object things visible and comprehensible; Faith, things which are invisible and even incomprehensible. Knowledge is founded on experience, on

---

for the dead, and of both for the whole Church, is to the Russian the bond which links together the Church in one Communion of Saints. We are not now discussing the evidence and authority for this custom of invocation, nor how far it is beneficial. What is necessary is to realise that this is very different from the more developed forms of Adoration of the Saints.

[1] *Catechism*, Blackmore, p. 88.

examination of its object ; but Faith, on belief of testimony
to truth. Knowledge belongs partly to the intellect, although
it may also act on the heart; Faith belongs principally to
the heart, although it is imparted through the intellect.'

On Faith and Works, the Catechism teaches as
follows :—

'*Q.* What should be the effect and fruit of true faith in the
Christian ?

'*A. Charity* or *love*, and *good works* conformable thereto.

'*Q.* Is not faith alone enough for a Christian, *without love
and good works* ?

'*A.* No ; for faith without love and good works is inactive
and dead, and so cannot lead to eternal life.

'*Q.* May not a man on the other hand be saved by love and
good works, *without faith* ?

'*A.* It is impossible that a man who has not faith in God
should really love Him ; besides, man, being ruined
by sin, cannot do really good works, unless he receive
through faith in Jesus Christ spiritual strength, or
grace from God.

'*Q.* What is to be thought of such love as *is not accompanied
by good works* ?

'*A.* Such love is not real : for true love naturally shows
itself by good works.'[1]

On the Scriptures and Tradition, the teaching in the
Duty of Priests is :—

'Since the Articles of the Faith and the Law of the Ten
Commandments are contained in Holy Scripture, as afore-
said, it follows, beyond dispute, that we hold the Word of
God, that is, the books of the Old and New Testaments, as

---

[1] *The Longer Catechism*, Blackmore, pp. 118-119.

the source, foundation, and perfect rule both of our holy
Faith, and of the good works of the Law. *Wherefore it is our
duty to search the Word of God, and draw from it divine truth,
to teach the people ; and to confirm our own words from the Word
of God ; and to this test to bring all doctrine, which either we ourselves may hear from others, or others from us, receiving what is
agreeable thereto, and rejecting what is contrary.'*

'The writings of the holy Fathers are of great use : for
they contain either the very same articles of the faith explained from the Word of God ; or instructions serviceable
for holy living; or else canons and rules for the discipline
and good order of the Church, and of the whole Christian
community, which we call traditions ecclesiastical. Wherefore we both may, and on occasion ought, in our discourses to
quote from the writings of the holy Fathers also such
passages as may be suitable for the explanation of any
article of faith, or for confirmation of our doctrine delivered
to the people. But neither the writings of the holy Fathers,
nor the traditions of the Church, are to be confounded or
equalled with the Word of God, and His commandments ; *for
the Word of God is one thing ; but the writings of the holy Fathers,
and traditions ecclesiastical, are another.'* [1]

I will give one more extract, this time from the
writings of Khomiakoff, which will, I think, suggest the
teaching of his Church :—

'The Spirit of God, who lives in the Church, ruling her
and making her wise, manifests Himself within her in divers
manners; in Scripture, in tradition, and in works; for the
Church, which does the works of God, is the same Church
which preserves tradition, and which has written the Scriptures. Neither individuals, nor a multitude of individuals
within the Church, preserve tradition or write the Scriptures ; but the Spirit of God, which lives in the whole body
of the Church. Therefore it is neither right nor possible to

---

[1] *Duty of Parish Priests*, pp. 161, 164.

look for the grounds of tradition in the Scriptures, nor for the proof of Scripture in tradition, nor for the warrant of Scripture or tradition in works. To a man living outside the Church, neither her Scripture nor her tradition nor her works are comprehensible. But to the man who lives within the Church and is united to the spirit of the Church, their unity is manifest by the grace which lives within her.' [1]

I have now, I think, given quite enough extracts to illustrate the teaching of the Russian Church on different doctrines, and must conclude this part of my subject with some more or less general observations.

1. In the first place, what is quite clear about the Russian Church, as of the Eastern Church as a whole, is that it represents a natural and organic development. A Russian monk once said to me, speaking of the Reformation, ' You, you have changed things; we have never changed anything from the days of the Apostles.' The statement is, of course, in its extreme form, untrue, but in another sense it is perfectly true; there has never, or only in smaller matters, been any deliberate change. The growth and modification has been natural, unconscious, and organic. The Eastern Church has never been in the position of having to make a selection, so to speak, of what it will accept or reject; it has never reconstructed and recast its teaching. An historian, looking over long periods, can notice changes. He can, perhaps, date the first appearance of this or that custom; the modifications of the first three centuries may be a matter of dispute, but a great

---

transforming influence like scholasticism, or the Reformation, or the Council of Trent, the Eastern Church has never known.

2. And this leads us to a second point. The Church of Russia has never been influenced, except in details, by the whole development of Western Theology, from St. Augustine onwards. It preserves for us the tone and the spirit and the thought of the Church of St. Chrysostom and St. Athanasius. That this is altogether a gain, I should be the last to assert. The first great break in Christian unity was of infinite harm to the Church, as all breaks have been, for it cut off the East from the active religious thought of the West, and it took away any check that might have existed to what all will probably recognise as the one-sided development of Western thought. The West has retained and intensified a heightened sense of the individual life, of the reality of sin, of the necessity of personal conversion; it has lost, in the introduction into all theology, whether Roman or Protestant, of hard, legal ideas, of a too rigid system, of an exaggerated desire for construction, of a banishment of mystery, of the attempt to solve, by human reason, problems which are quite inexplicable. The early Councils anathematised those who added to the creeds. The Eastern Church sometimes dates the disunion of Christendom to the time when the Western Church added the *Filioque*. At any rate, an importation of philosophy into religious belief, and an attempt at precision in many questions where precision is impossible, has burdened us with creeds, and articles of religion which are treated almost as

creeds, and which certainly subject all the different
Churches to the anathema pronounced at the Council
of Ephesus against those who added articles to the
Christian faith.

3. We shall find that a Russian theologian will tell
us that we in the West always look at everything
through Roman spectacles. Either we have received
our doctrines straight from Rome, or have developed
them in opposition to a Roman point of view. There
is, they would tell us—and tell us with truth—an older,
and a different point of view, from which they look at
things. They are not troubled with the conflict between Scripture and tradition, for both alike are part
of the teaching of the Church; the Bible is a part of
tradition, and tradition is in the Bible. They do not ask
whether a man in justified by faith or by works, as the
antithesis of the two is to them impossible. 'When we
ask, "Can true faith save without works?" we ask a
senseless question; or, better to say, no question at all.
If the faith is a living faith which does works, it is faith
in Christ, and Christ in faith.'

Enough has been said about the teaching of the Russian
Church and about its doctrinal attitude. It has, of
course, been necessary to touch only on some points,
but I hope that what has been said will not only have
elucidated those special points, but also will have given
some idea of the mental attitude of the Russian Church
as a whole. I must add now a few words on the ex-
ternal side of the Russian Church life. A very unjust
and one-sided estimate is often taken of this.

The historical development of the Russian people

has been different from our own, they are of a different race and character, and in civilisation they started many centuries later than we did. Their religion, again, is in many ways different, but no one can doubt its intense reality and power. One of the elements of power and stability in Russia is the hold religion and the National Church have on the great mass of the people. The universal belief in miracles, the veneration of the Eikons, and the passion for pilgrimages, are all signs of this devotion, and help in turn to educate and foster the religious feeling. There are few contrasts greater than that of passing from a Greek monastery on Mount Athos to the great Russian houses. There is no sight in Palestine more impressive than that of the devotion and enthusiasm and endurance of the Russian pilgrims.

There are three characteristics of the Russian Church that I should like to dwell on somewhat longer. The first is, that it is a National Church. One of the characteristics of the Eastern Church has been that it has apparently so far solved the problem of combining in Christian unity national churches, and of identifying the National Church with the life of the nation without leading to its separation from other bodies. Foremost among these churches, certainly the largest National Church in the world, is that of Russia, with perhaps 80,000,000 of adherents. It is a National Church, and it has been bound up in an especial way with the fortunes of the country. In the great struggle with the Tartars, it was round the Church that the defence rallied, and some of the monasteries were the great fortresses of resistance against a foreign invader. So, too, the unique position of the Tzar in the Church, however it be defined, and however it be justified, is a sign of the identification of the Church and the nation, and the nation with the Church.

Then, secondly, the Russian Church is the Church of the laity. The theoretical side of this has been referred to in what was said of the place of the laity in the Church. The Eastern Church, and especially the Russian, considers that to the whole body of the Church—laity as well as clergy—belongs the Divine Spirit, working through faith and love, which preserves the Church from error. Practically, this fact is brought out by the extent to which the religious life of the people never requires, as so often in this country, to be kept alive by the energy of the clergy. The drunken village pope has become a typical character in fiction—and unfortunately he is not unknown in real life—but if, in England, the parson is immoral or incompetent, the church is deserted; in Russia, the pope is compelled by the people to perform the ministrations which he alone can do. Their religion comes from themselves, and they are taught it as part of the traditions which they inherit.

And then, thirdly, if we were to try and sum up the distinguishing features of the Russian Church—just as we might say that one great characteristic of the English Church was practical philanthropy, or of Germany a devotion to theological study, or of Scotland a taste for metaphysical and theological discussion—so of Russia we might say that it was religious devotion. There may be superstition, although that is a word the meaning of which, except as a term of abuse, is very difficult to fix; there is probably in many cases an insufficient grasp of the connection between morality and religion, but of the deep religious devotion of the people there can be no doubt. It is strong, simple, deep, and makes Russia a more formidable power, under certain circumstances, than we are inclined to believe, or than perhaps many of its own rulers realise. The half-religious, half-political movement which presses Russia over southwards to the holy places, is one of the forces which will mould history in the future much more surely than the skill of its statesmen. Russia is a religious power not to be despised, one of the great factors which will mould the religion of the future. What, then, are its relations to England and the Anglican Church?

This is not a very easy question to answer, for it must be remembered that in Russia, as in England and as in Rome, there are two points of view. Just as with us there are Bishops who write—as one wrote to me—'that he considered the whole Eastern Church to be so corrupt and idolatrous, that the less contact we have with it the better,' so, not long ago, a Russian Bishop in America wrote: 'Who, then, belongs to this One, Holy, Catholic and Apostolic Church? . . . Only the Eastern Churches (remain) in the fold—the four Patriarchates of Constantinople, Alexandria, Antioch, and Jerusalem; the Churches of Russia, Greece, Georgia, Roumania, some Slavic countries, and others now known under the name of Orthodox.' 'All the Western Christians, on

the other hand—the Roman Catholic Church and all
the Protestant communities, sprung out of the bosom
of this Church: Anglican, Episcopalian, Lutheran,
Calvinist, etc.—all these do not belong to the One Holy
Catholic Church.' . . . 'The Anglican Church, besides
distorting the doctrine of the Sacraments and other
dogmas, cannot even, so far, prove her hierarchy's
claim to direct Apostolic succession, while other sects
have no trace at all of hierarchy or of Sacraments.'
And then he goes on very clearly, 'But it may be that
some persons will ask: "Is salvation possible in these
Christian communities? Can it really be that it is not?"
To this we answer directly and decisively that it is not.'

I have made this quotation in order to make it clear
that there are extreme men in the Russian Church as
there are in the English, and I shall have to refer to it
again in conclusion. I may state definitely that this is
not the feeling of the Russian Church as a whole, and
the teaching implied is incorrect. It is perfectly true
that the Eastern Church considers that it alone is the
true Church, excluding the Roman Catholics quite as
much as ourselves, but its writers are careful to guard
against condemning those outside its own body.

'Inasmuch as the earthly and visible Church is not the
fulness and completeness of the whole Church which the
Lord has appointed to appear at the final judgment of all
creation, she acts and knows only within her own limits; and
(according to the words of Paul the Apostle to the Corin-
thians, 1 Cor. v. 12), does not judge the rest of mankind, and
only looks upon those as excluded, that is to say, not belonging to her, who exclude themselves. The rest of mankind.
whether alien from the Church, or united to her by ties

which God has not willed to reveal to her, she leaves to the judgment of the great day. The Church on earth judges for herself only, according to the grace of the Spirit, and the freedom granted her through Christ, inviting also the rest of mankind to the unity and adoption of God in Christ; but upon those who do not hear her appeal she pronounces no sentence, knowing the command of her Saviour and Head, "not to judge another man's servant."[1]

Again, we should, I think, remember that although not so hard or rigid as the Roman Church, and resenting its attitude very much, the Eastern Church in its very nature is certainly more immobile. That arises really, I believe, from the fact that it has, as I have said, hardly ever made any conscious change; that it represents, in a way which no Western Church can, an organic growth. So diplomatic arrangement of doctrines will do no good in dealing with Russia, whatever might be the case with Rome.

'The Church has in itself nothing of a State, and can admit of nothing like a conditional union. It is quite a different case with the Church of Rome. She is a State, . . . and has a right to act as a State. Union is possible with Rome. Unity alone is possible with Orthodoxy.'[2]

I have stated these facts definitely, because it seems to me necessary. As soon as the recent decision of the Pope on Anglican Orders had been published, I began to receive letters from Colonial bishops and others, to the effect that as the Church of Rome had rejected us, I should take immediate steps for our reunion with the East, while I read a letter in the paper from a

---

[1] Khomiakoff, in *Russia and the English Church*, vol. i. p. 194.
[2] *Russia and the English Church*, vol. i. p. 8.

distinguished English Prelate, saying we should take
steps to be reunited with the Presbyterian Church of
Scotland. There seemed to be something intensely
unpractical and decidedly undignified in these letters.
It was rather like a woman who, having failed to secure
the attentions of one suitor, should advertise to the
world her desire to get another.

You will never heal the divisions in the body of
Christ by methods such as these; you will never thus
bring to an end differences which are the result not
only of doctrinal dispute, but of deep-seated diversity of
character and history, and have been intensified by
centuries of estrangement. The attempt at reunion
would be only too likely to bring to the front the
extremer sections on either side, just as, recently, we
have had the doctrines of the Roman Church re-stated
for us by a Cardinal whose language is not only un-
attractive to English Churchmen, but also would be
looked upon as extreme by a large number of members
of his own community, and those the most learned;
while I ask you, as sensible men, is our own Church
sufficiently educated to make a proposal for reunion
in any way practical?

If we are to aim at reunion, our method must be
different; it must be one which works without caring
for the immediate results, one which works by the sober
path of theological study, of mutual intercourse and
charity, of educating both ourselves and others.

The immediate practical conclusion that I wish you
to draw is: To realise the existence of the Russian
Church as a great fact in religion, and as a great

witness in Christian theology. Rome bulks very large in the eyes of some of us. It is at hand, and we are conscious of it. It is a good thing that we should realise that there is another Church which, on historical grounds, has as great, or even greater claims to represent the Catholic teaching of the undivided Church,—that, in many points, it bears a living witness against the teaching of the Roman Church, and that in all these points it is on the side of our own Church. We cannot, with the Eastern Church before our eyes, believe that the claim the Church of Rome makes to be the one Church, is true. Every historian knows that these claims are untenable in history; the existence of the Eastern Church is an object-lesson to the truth of history. We, as English churchmen, appeal to an undivided Church; when the Church is—if it be God's will—once more united, then we shall receive and accept the testimony of that united body.

And a very definite work is before us. We have to do what our position helps us very much to do, to build up a sober exposition of Catholic truth, both historical and scientific. We have much sympathy in doing so from many outside our body. Even fifty years ago, Khomiakoff wrote: ‘England, with its modest science and its serious love of religious truth, might seem to give some hope.’ It is our reverent criticism which has attracted the best minds of the Roman Church.

We must remember that to be Catholic does not mean to revive this or that mediæval custom, or adopt this or that formula. It means to realise the Catholic faith in all its breadth and freedom. To understand that it is a body of truth which illustrates and is illustrated by every side of truth and knowledge. We must learn to be more historical, and more scientific, and because we are both, more Catholic. And then, when we look on the practical side, we have to realise that our own Church, to deserve her name Catholic, should be truly and in reality, what it is to only a certain extent at present, the Church of the Nation, and the Church of the Empire.

To perform these two tasks, we must learn to combine loyalty to our own Church, with charity towards other Christian bodies. Charity without loyalty is a mere name. We must believe in our own Church, but not allow that belief to make us rigid or narrow. Sober research, earnest work, loyalty, charity, prayer—these are the methods by which we can advance the Reunion of Christendom.

APPENDIX

A. Service Books of the Russian Church.—The services of the Russian Church are for the most part identical with those of other branches of the Greek Church, and the service books are largely the same, but translated into the Old Slavonic or Church Language. The services may be divided into

(1) The Liturgy.

(2) The Daily Offices.

(3) The Occasional Offices, Rites, and Ceremonies.

The following are the principal books required:

1. *Tipikon* (Gr. τυπικόν), the book of the rules and regulations to determine the service for the seasons and days of the year. The services and directions are both often very complicated.

2. *Sloujebnik* (Gr. Λειτουργικόν). This contains the text of the three Liturgies of St. Basil, St. Chrysostom, and the Presanctified. This must be supplemented, however, by the books containing the Deacons' portion and the Fixed Hymns, while the variable portions are given in the books mentioned below.

3. *Trebnik* (Book of Needs) or Euchologion. This contains most of the occasional sacraments and rites, and also generally the fixed portions of the Liturgy.

4. *Tshasoslow*, in Greek Ὡρολόγιον, contains the Canonical Hours.

5. The *Lections* are usually contained in three separate volumes with the Ἐυαγγελιστήριον or table of lessons.

6. The variable portions of the service are contained in the *Octoich* (Ὀκτώηχος), containing the variable hymns for Sundays, the *Triod* (Τριώδιον), those for Lent and the three preceding weeks, the *Pentakostariy* (πεντηκοστάριον) those for Easter, and the *Mineya* (Μηναῖα), the immovable feasts.

Brightman, *Liturgies*, lxxxii; King, *Rites, etc.*, p. 42; Neale, p. 819.

B. The three *Liturgies* in use are—

(1) The Byzantine Liturgy of St. Chrysostom, the Liturgy in ordinary use.

(2) The Byzantine Liturgy of St. Basil, used upon all the Sundays of the Great Fast, except Palm Sunday; upon Holy Thursday, the vigils of Christmas and Epiphany, and St. Basil's day.

(3) The Liturgy of St. Gregory Dialogos, or of the Presanctified, used on Wednesdays and Fridays in the Great Fast.

A complete and scholarly edition of the Greek texts of St. Chrysostom and St. Basil is given in Brightman, *Oriental Liturgies*, pp. 353, 411. The Greek use differs only in a few rubrics from the Slavonic. Full accounts of these Liturgies are given in Neale, with translations.

C. The Canonical Hours.—There are eight canonical hours, but prayers are actually said three times daily. Matins (Μεσονυκτικὸν), Lauds (Ὄρθρον), and Prime, being said early in the morning; Tierce, Sext, and the Liturgy later; Nones, Vespers (Ἑσπερινὸν or *wetshernya*), and Compline (ἀπόδειπνον) in the evening. Neale, p. 894; King, p. 123.

D. The *Occasional Offices* are very numerous, including all that is implied by both the *Rituale* and *Pontificale* in Latin, and also a large number of Domestic Offices.

E. Translations into English :—

KING, *Rites and Ceremonies of the Greek Church in Russia*, London, 1772.

This is the only translation made from the Russian. It contains the Liturgies of St. Chrysostom and the Pre-sanctified, the Daily Offices, and most of the Occasional Offices, including the ordination services.

NEALE, *History of the Holy Eastern Church*, vols. i. and ii., London, 1850.

Contains descriptions and translations of the Liturgy, and much information, with translations, of the other offices.

NEALE, *The Divine Liturgy of our father among the Saints*, *John Chrysostom.* London, 1860.

ROBERTSON, αἱ θεῖαι λειτουργίαι : *the Divine Liturgies.* London, 1894.

SHANN, *Euchology.* Contains a large number of the Daily Offices. London, 1894.

SHANN, *Book of Needs.* Contains many of the Occasional Offices. London, 1894.

F. Doctrinal Statements of the Eastern Church.—As has been explained above (p. 3) no document has symbolical authority except the Creed. The theology of the Russian Church is based on the Canons of the seven general councils and on the fathers, especially the *De Fide Orthodoxa* of St. John of Damascus. The chief modern authoritative documents are the following :—

1. *The Answers of the Patriach Jeremiah to the Lutherans.*
   These have not apparently ever been translated into the Russian, or published there with authority.

2. *The Orthodox Confessions of the Faith of the Catholic and Apostolic Church of the East.*—This was written by Peter Mogila, Metropolitan of Kieff, 1632-47.

'If it be asked how much weight is to be attached
to the Orthodox Confession, we answer that besides all
that we have related above of the care taken originally
in its composition and revision, and of its approval
both by the Synod of Jassy, and by the four Eastern
Patriarchs, it received afterwards the testimonies of
Nectarius, Patriarch of Constantinople, . . . of
Dositheus, Patriarch of Jerusalem, with his Synod
held at Bethlehem in 1672; also at the same time of
Dionysius, Patriarch of Constantinople; again in
1691, that of a Synod held at Constantinople; and
lastly in 1696, that of Adrian, Patriarch of Moscow.
It is acknowledged by the Spiritual Regulations
subscribed by the bishops and clergy of Russia in the
year 1720, and all Russian theologians since have
rested very much on this book.' (Blackmore, p. xxv.)

3. *The XVIII Articles of the Synod of Bethlehem.*—The
Synod was held in 1672. The articles seem to have
been communicated to the Russian Church in 1721,
and published in an authorised Russian translation,
which differs in many points from the Greek, in 1838.
(See *Neale,* p. 1173). The Greek may be found in
Hardouin's *Concil.,* xi. p. 180.

Both the above documents are somewhat tinged
with Latin teaching.

4. *The Longer Catechism.*—This in its present form was
drawn up by Philaret, Archbishop of Moscow. It was
adopted by the Holy Synod in 1839, and sent to all
the Eastern Patriarchs, and to other churches of the
same rite and communion. Translated by Blackmore
(see below).

5. *The Treatise on the Duty of Parish Priests.*—Composed by
George Konissky, Bishop of Mogileff, with the assist-
ance of Parthenius Sopkofsky, Bishop of Smolensk.
It was first printed at St. Petersburg, A.D. 1776.
It has been adopted by the whole Russian Church;

and all candidates for holy orders in the Diocesan Seminaries and in the Superior Spiritual Academies are required to have read it. Translated by Blackmore.

6. To these we may add the declaration of Faith made by a bishop at his consecration. It is translated by King, p. 293.

G. Translations of Doctrinal Works :—

BLACKMORE, *The Doctrine of the Russian Church.* Aberdeen, 1845.

Contents.—The Primer or Spelling Book ; The Shorter and Longer Catechisms ; The Duty of Parish Priests.

H. Some Works on the Russian Church.

KING, *The Rites and Ceremonies of the Greek Church in Russia.* London, 1772.

NEALE, *A History of the Holy Eastern Church.* London, 1850.

ROMANOFF, *Sketches of the Rites and Customs of the Graeco-Russian Church.* London, 1869. (Popular.)

KHOMIAKOFF, *L'Eglise Latine et le Protestantisme au point de vue de l'Eglise d'Orient.* Lausanne and Vevey, 1872.

BIRKBECK, *Russia and the English Church during the last fifty years.* London, 1895. Published for the Eastern Church Association.

STANLEY, *Lectures on the Eastern Church.* London, 1862.

MACAIRE, *Introduction à la Théologie Orthodoxe,* 1857-59.

MOURAVIEFF, *History of the Church of Russia.* Translated by Blackmore, 1842.

Eastern Church Association.

OBJECTS OF THE ASSOCIATION.

(1) To give information as to the state and position of the Eastern Christians, in order gradually to better their condition through the influence of public opinion.

(2) To make known to the Christians of the East the doctrine and principles of the Anglican Church.

(3) To take advantage of all opportunities which the Providence of God shall afford for Intercommunion with the Orthodox Church, and also for friendly intercourse with the other ancient Churches of the East.

(4) To assist, as far as possible, the Bishops of the Orthodox Church in their efforts to promote the spiritual welfare and the education of their flocks.

STANDING COMMITTEE.

The Right Rev. the BISHOP OF READING (*Chairman*), Christ Church, Oxford.

The Very Rev. the DEAN OF ST. PAUL'S.

Rev. N. T. GARRY, Hon. Canon of Christ Church, Oxford.

Rev. W. C. E. NEWBOLT, Canon of St. Paul's, Amen Court, London, E.C.

Rev. T. A. LACEY, Madingley Rectory, Cambridge.

Rev. S. J. M. PRICE, St. Ive's Vicarage, Hunts.

Rev. R. MILBURN BLAKISTON, 7 Dean's Yard, Westminster, S.W.

Rev. F. E. BRIGHTMAN, Pusey House, St. Giles', Oxford.

Sir THEODORE C. HOPE, K.C.S.I., C.I.E., 21 Elvaston Place, S.W.

Sir JOHN CONROY, Bart., Fellow of Balliol College, Oxford.

G. W. E. RUSSELL, Esq., 18 Wilton Street, S.W.

W. J. BIRKBECK, Esq., 32 Sloane Gardens, S.W.

C. R. FREEMAN, Esq., 20 Gutter Lane, Cheapside.

EDWIN FRESHFIELD, Esq., LL.D., 35 Russell Square, W.C.

ATHELSTAN RILEY, Esq., 2 Kensington Court, W.

C. KNIGHT WATSON, Esq., F.S.A., 49 Bedford Square, W.C.

H. O. WAKEMAN, Esq., Fellow of All Souls' College, Oxford.

Treasurer—G. T. BIDDULPH, Esq., 43 Charing Cross.

Secretary—Rev. A. C. HEADLAM, The Rectory, Welwyn, Herts.

Assistant Secretary—Miss GOODWIN, Saltwood Rectory, Hythe, Kent.

Any one desirous of becoming a Member is requested to communicate with the Assistant Secretary.